# Some fascinating avian eggs

Kurt Schläpfer

Dedicated to my wife Béatrice whose egg collection
inspired me to write this book.

# Table of content

## Preface

There are 11,000 bird species. Which of their eggs are fascinating? Extreme variations of eggs, e.g. the largest eggs, are always perceived as fascinating, and this even more, if the largest eggs belong to extinct birds. Particularly fascinating are very colorful eggs, which is typical for the tinamu eggs, or eggs with an extraordinary shape, such as the egg of the Common Murre. Moreover, it is fascinating when the same bird lays eggs of very different appearance. This applies to brood parasites such as the Common Cuckoo. The fascinating aspect of penguin eggs is that some species lay eggs of very different size (egg size diphormism). And the size of kiwi eggs is fascinating in relation to the size of the female bird.

In contrast to other publications on avian eggs, this book provides detailed data of the described eggs in terms of length, width, volume and weight.

August 2018                                                    Kurt Schläpfer

# 1. The largest avian eggs

---

*The largest avian eggs have to be found among the extinct bird species. There are about 20 extinct bird species that have (probably) laid larger eggs than the largest extant bird, the Common Ostrich. However, only a small part of these eggs are known. This chapter describes the eggs of 12 extinct bird species.*

**What is a large egg?**
Avian eggs span a weight-range between 0.25 g and 1.6 kg. For this study, it is arbitrarily defined that an egg mass of at least 0.5 kg can be described as large. Among the 11,000 extant bird species, there are only four species laying eggs of this size. These are:
- the Ostrich (*Struthio camelus*)
- the Greater Rhea (*Rhea americana*)
- the Cassowary (*Casuarius casuarius*)
- the Emu (*Dromaius novaehollandiae*)

These four bird species belong to a group of flightless birds called ratites. Extant flying birds are not able to produce such large eggs. The largest egg laid by a flying bird belongs to the Wandering Albatross (*Diomedea exulans*) weighing 455 grams. Considerably larger bird eggs are found among the extinct bird species.

**The largest extinct bird species**
There are essentially six bird families which include the largest birds that have ever lived:

*Gastornithidae:*
This family includes eight species with one famous representative, the *Gastornis giganteus* from which some eggshell characteristics are known.

*Phorusrhacidae (terror birds):*
The largest group of extinct giant birds are the terror birds.
Many of the 18 species reached a body mass of over 100 kg
(ALVARENGA 2003). The largest bird of this family was the
*Brontornis burmeisteri*, which weighed up to 400 kg. The
second largest species of the terror birds was the *Kelenken
guillermoi* with a body mass of 225 kg. The eggs of these
birds are not known.

*Table 1: An incomplete list of extinct giant birds*
*(sorted by bird body mass)*

| Family | Species | Bird height m | Bird body mass kg | Eggshell findings |
|---|---|---|---|---|
| Dromornithidae | Dromornis stirtoni | 3.0 | 500 | x |
| Aepyornithidae | Aepyornis maximus | 2.8 | 450 | x |
| Phorusrhacidae | Brontornis burmeisteri | 2.8 | 375 | |
| Dinornithidae | Dinornis robustus | 3.7 | 300 | x |
| Dromornithidae | Dromornis planei | 2.5 | 300 | |
| Dromornithidae | Bullockornis planei | 2.4 | 300 | |
| Dromornithidae | Genyornis newtoni | 2.2 | 275 | x |
| Phorusrhacidae | Kelenken guillermoi | 2.6 | 225 | |
| Dromornithidae | Dromornis australis | 2.2 | 220 | |
| Dinornithidae | Dinornis novaezealandidae | 3.0 | 200 | x |
| Dinornithidae | Pachyornis elephantopus | 1.2 | 190 | x |
| Phorusrhacidae | Paraphysornis brasiliensis | 2.4 | 180 | |
| Dromornithidae | Ilbandornis woodburnei | 1.9 | 175 | |
| Gastornithidae | Gastornis giganteus | 2.6 | 160 | x |
| Phorusrhacidae | Devincenzia pozzi | 2.5 | 160 | |
| Dromornithidae | Ilbandornis lawsoni | 1.9 | 150 | |
| Incerta sedis | Gargantuavis philoinos | 1.7 | 140 | |
| Phorusrhacidae | Titanis walleri | 2.5 | 135 | |
| Phorusrhacidae | Phorusrhacos longissimus | 2.4 | 130 | |

| Family | Species | Bird height m | Bird body mass kg | Eggshell findings |
|---|---|---|---|---|
| *Gastornithidae* | *Gastornis parisiensis* | | 120 | |
| *Dinornithidae* | *Euryapterix gravis* | 3.1 | 110 | x |
| *Teratornithidae* | *Argentavis magnificens* | 1.7 | 80 | |
| *Dinornithidae* | *Emeus crassus* | 0.8 | 70 | x |
| *Dromornithidae* | *Barawertornis tedfordi* | 0.7 | 70 | |
| *Phorusrhacidae* | *Mesembriornis milneedwardsi* | 1.5 | 70 | |
| *Phorusrhacidae* | *Andalgalornis steulleti* | 1.4 | 70 | |
| *Sylviornithidae* | *Sylviornis neocaledoniae* | 1.4 | 40 | |
| *Dinornithidae* | *Megalapteryx didinus* | 0.7 | 38 | x |
| *Dinornithidae* | *Anomalopteryx didiformis* | 1.3 | 35 | x |
| *Phorusrhacidae* | *Patagornis marshi* | 1.7 | 35 | |
| *Dinornithidae* | *Euryapterix curtus* | 0.7 | 34 | x |

*Dromornithidae (thunderbirds):*
The (probably) largest bird that has ever lived belongs to the family of thunderbirds. It is the Stirton Thunderbird (*Dromornis stirtoni*), which weighed 500 kg. Another heavyweight member of this family is the *Genyornis newtoni* with an estimated body mass of 275 kg (MURRAY 2004, RICH 1979). From these two bird species some eggshell data are available (see next section).


*Teratornithidae:*
This family includes the probably largest flying bird, the *Argentavis magnificens* weighing about 70 kg. Eggshell data of this bird species are not known, but it can be estimated that its eggs must have had a weight of about 1 kg (PALMQVIST 2003, CHATTERJEE 2007).

*Dinornithidae (moa birds):*
The best documented family of large birds are the moa birds (KRÖSCHE 2006, ANDERSON 2010, WORTHY 2002) which have been extinct since about 600 years. The largest member of this family is the Giant Moa (*Dinornis robustus*), which was the tallest (but not the heaviest) of all birds. Eggshell characteristics are described for eight of the nine species of moa birds.

*Figure 1: Three of the largest birds compared to the size of a standing man*
*From left: Great Elephantbird (Aepyornis maximus), Giant Moa (Dinornis giganteus), Stirton Thunderbird (Dromornis stirtoni)*

*Aepyornithidae (elephantbirds):*
From the family of elephantbirds only one species lived until the last millennium, the Great Elephantbird *Aepyornis maximus*. Of this bird, about one hundred eggs are preserved.

Apart from the bird families mentioned above, there are other extinct species falling into the category of large birds (see table 1). But no eggshell characteristics are known.

As to the body mass of the birds listed in table 1, these data are subject to great uncertainties, because they are mostly extrapolations based on bone dimensions (NGUYEN 2010, WORTHY 2017, ANGST 2015, HANDLEY 2016). Therefore, the question, which was the largest bird of all times, cannot be clearly answered.

**The largest (known) avian eggs**

Of the dinosaurs that became extinct 65 million years ago, hundreds of thousands of eggs have been found. It is therefore surprising that of the extinct birds discussed here, which have lived much longer, mostly poor eggshell data are available. The author of this article was only able to collect eggshell data of twelve extinct species (see table 2), nine of which being extinct since less than 600 years.

The most interesting giant bird is the Stirton Thunderbird. However, information about its eggs is scarse and not very consistent (MURRAY 2004). As no larger parts of eggs were found, the egg size has been extrapolated from small fragments. Information about three egg sizes can be found which are very different. The calculated weight of the smallest of the three eggs is 7 kg, which has to be considered too low. The second egg weighs 10.2 kg, which seems plausible compared to eggs of comparable birds. Only small fragments of the third egg were found. From the curvature of these fragments it was calculated that the egg could have had a length of 32 to 42 cm and a width of 24 to 29 cm. Taking the mean value of 37 × 26.5, a weight of 16.6 kg can be calculated, which is an improbable value (see section after next).

The second species of thunderbirds for which eggshell data are available is the *Genyornis newtoni*. Egg dimensions have been calculated from shell fragments, which suggest an egg weight of 1.4 kg (ANGST 2014). This egg size appears rather small compared to the almost equally heavy Giant Moa, which laid three times larger eggs. The *Genyornis newtoni* is also attributed an egg (see figure 2) whose fragments were found in 2001 and which has been almost completely reconstructed (GRELLET-TINNER 2016). However, with a weight of under 0.8 kg this egg is most likely not an egg of the *Genyornis newtoni*. Based on the assumed body mass of 275 kg, the egg of *Genyornis newtoni* should have a weight of at least 2.8 kg.

*Fig. 2: Reconstructed egg of an unknown large bird:*
*The eggshell fragments were found by Nigel Spooner in Australia in 2001. It is therefore referred to as "Spooner egg". The age was dated 55,000 years. The calculated fresh weight is 0.676 kg.*

In the family of the terror birds (*Gastornithidae*), eggshell fragments are only described for the *Gastornis giganteus* (BUFFETAUT 2008). This bird species has been extinct since about 40 million years. The shell fragments were found in sediment layers. Two different egg sizes were calculated. From this it can be determined that the egg weight must have been about 1.4 kg.

In the group of moa birds (*Dinornithidae*), most probably all nine species have laid eggs weighing more than 0.5 kg. There are descriptions of 36 eggs which can be assigned to eight species (GILL 2006 and 2007). From the dimensions of these eggs it can be calculated that their weight ranges from 0.53 kg to 4.5 kg (see table 2).

The best documented eggs belong to the Great Elephantbird (*Aepyornis maximus*). The author of this article was able to collect data on 63 eggs of this bird species (SCHLÄPFER 2017). Therefore, the calculated average egg weight of 9.34 kg is statistically reliable. (The *Aepyornis* egg is described in greater detail in Chapter 2.)

*Figure 3: Moa eggs*
*1 Dinornis robustus (Giant Moa)*
*2 Pachyornis elephantopus*
*3 Euryapteryx gravis*
*4 Dinornis novaezealandiae*
*5 Emeus crassus*
*6 Anomalopteryx didiformis*
*7 Megalapteryx didinus*

In table 2, the egg weight of the Great Elephantbird ranks behind the egg weight of the Stirton Thunderbird. However, this egg weight is – compared to the egg of the elephant bird – an unreliable estimate. If this egg size is compared with the largest egg known from the Great Elephantbird weighing 12.3 kg, it seems clear that the Great Elephantbird laid the largest eggs of all time.

Of the extant birds only four species lay eggs weighing more than 0.5 kg. While the weight of three species does not exceed 0.66 kg, the Common Ostrich (*Struthio camelus*) lays eggs about three times as heavy (SCHÖNWETTER 1960-92).

*Figure 4: The largest eggs of extant birds compared to a chicken egg:*
*Top left: Common Ostrich (Struthio camelus)*
*Top right: Cassowary (Casuarius casuarius):*
*Below left: Greater Rhea (Rhea americana)*
*Below center: Emu (Dromaius novaehollandiae)*

*Table 2: Egg data of some giant birds*



| | Egg length mm | Egg width mm | Egg volume ml | Egg mass g | Shell thickness mm |
|---|---|---|---|---|---|
| *Aepyornis maximus* | 306 | 225 | 8118 | 9336 | 3.3 |
| *Dromornis stirtoni* | 276<br>290<br>370 | 207<br>240<br>265 | 6150<br>8686<br>13,511 | 7094<br>10,240<br>16,578 | 3.5 |
| *Dinornis robustus* | 240 | 178 | 3954 | 4474 | 3.7 |
| *Genyornis newtoni* | 155<br>126 | 125<br>97 | 1260<br>616 | 1392<br>676 | 1.15 |
| *Dinornis novaezealandiae* | 190 | 150 | 2223 | 2477 | 3.0 |
| *Pachyornis elephantopus* | 230 | 170 | 3456 | 3893 | 1.56 |
| *Gastornis giganteus* | 178<br>240 | 120<br>100 | 1333<br>1248 | 1466<br>1378 | 2.4 |
| *Struthio camelus* | 153 | 135 | 1445 | 1600 | 1.92 |
| *Euryapterix gravis* | 207 | 145 | 2263 | 2522 | 1.43 |
| *Emeus crassus* | 179 | 134 | 1671 | 1853 | 1.0 |
| *Casuarius casuarius* | 137 | 92 | 603 | 662 | 0.97 |
| *Dromaius novaehollandiae* | 136 | 89 | 560 | 616 | 0.94 |
| *Anomalopteryx didiformis* | 172 | 120 | 1288 | 1423 | 1.19 |
| *Megalapteryx didinus* | 170 | 120 | 1273 | 1406 | 1.17 |
| *Rhea americana* | 126 | 86 | 485 | 532 | 0.91 |
| *Euryapterix curtus* | 121 | 97 | 592 | 650 | 0.90 |

## Egg weight as a function of bird weight

One might expect that the size of an egg is, in the broadest sense, correlated with the adult body mass of the animal hatching from that egg. If all oviparous animals are considered, however, the adult body mass is in no way related to its egg size. Example: Both the Common Eider (*Somateria mollissima*) and the Nile Crocodile (*Crocodylus niloticus*) lay an egg weighing about 110 grams. The adult eider duck weighs only about 2 kg, the Nile Crocodile, however, far more than 100 kg.

*Table 3: Egg mass in proportion to the adult body mass (sorted by bird body mass)*

| | Bird body mass kg | Egg mass g | Egg mass/ body mass % |
|---|---|---|---|
| *Dromornis stirtoni* | 500 | 10,240 | 2.05 |
| *Aepyornis maximus* | 450 | 9336 | 2.07 |
| *Dinornis robustus* | 300 | 4474 | 1.49 |
| *Genyornis newtoni* | 275 | 1392 | 0.51 |
| *Dinornis novaezealandiae* | 200 | 2477 | 1.24 |
| *Pachyornis elephantopus* | 190 | 3893 | 2.05 |
| *Gastornis giganteus* | 156 | 1466 | 1.08 |
| *Struthio camelus* | 156 | 1600 | 1.02 |
| *Euryapterix gravis* | 109 | 2522 | 2.31 |
| *Emeus crassus* | 70 | 1853 | 2.65 |
| *Casuarius casuarius* | 44 | 662 | 1.50 |
| *Dromaius* | 43 | 616 | 1.43 |
| *Megalapteryx didinus* | 38 | 1406 | 3.70 |
| *Anomalopteryx didiformis* | 35 | 1423 | 4.07 |
| *Euryapterix curtus* | 34 | 650 | 0.90 |
| *Rhea americana* | 23 | 532 | 2.31 |

For birds, the relationship between egg weight and adult body mass has been investigated in many publications (DICKISON 2007, RAHN 1975, DYKE 2010). In the opinion of the author of this book, there is no statistically reliable correlation between these two variables. One uncertainty is the adult body mass: Depending on the bird's health and nutritional status and the geographical origin of the population, the body mass can vary greatly. Experts belief that the error in case of body mass estimations is about ± 20% (MURRAY 2004). Moreover, birds of the same body mass can lay eggs of very different weights. For example, for a female body mass of 100 g, the egg weight can vary between 3.2 g and 25.4 g (SCHÖNWETTER 1985).

Even if only the egg weights above 0.5 kg are considered (see table 3), there is no clear evidence for a correlation with the bird body mass. The rule that, for eggs over 0.5 kg, the egg weight amounts to 1% to 2% of the female body mass, is valid only to a limited extent, as some species of the moa birds laid clearly heavier eggs.

**The upper size limit of an avian egg**
Although not all eggs of extinct animals are known, there is a strong probability that the Great Elephantbird laid the largest eggs of all animals with a maximum egg weight of 12.7 kg. The upper limit for the size of an animal egg is mainly determined by the eggshell thickness. The eggshell thickness increases in proportion to the egg weight. If the shell is too thin, the egg can break during oviposition or if the eggs are moved in the clutch. Moreover, the egg must be able to support the weight of the incubating animal. However, if the eggshell is too thick, the chick is no more able to break the shell with its own effort. In addition, the oxygen supply to the embryo is reduced with increasing eggshell thickness. Based on the physical laws for gas exchange, it is obvious that there must be an upper limit for the shell thickness which is estimated to be about 6 mm.

The largest average shell thickness was measured at an egg of the Great Elephantbird (*Aepyornis maximus*). This value is 5.85 mm (SCHÖNWETTER 1960). Since this egg has a weight of 12.7 kg, it can be estimated that – for a shell thickness of 6 mm – the maximum egg weight cannot be higher than approximately 14 kg.

# References


ANDERSON A. 2010: Prodigious Birds: Moas and Moa-Hunting in Prehistoric New Zealand. Cambridge University Press.

ANGST D., E. BUFFETAUT 2017: Paleobiology of Giant Flightless Birds. ISTE Press Ltd. London.

ANGST D. ET AL. 2014: Fossil avian eggs from the Palaeogene of southern France: new size estimates and a possible taxonomic identification of the egg-layer. Geol. Mag. 152: 70-79.

ALVARENGA H. M. F., E. HÖFLING 2003: Systematic Revision of the Phorusrhacidae (Aves: *Ralliformes*). Pap. Avuls Zool. 43(4), 2003 Volume 43(4):55-91.

BUFFETAUT E. 2008: First evidence of the giant bird *Gastornis* from southern Europe: a tibiotarsus from the Lower Eocene of Saint-Papoul. Oryctos Vol. 7, 75-82.

CHATTERJEE S. ET AL 2007: The aerodynamics of *Argentavis*, the world's largest flying bird from the Miocene of Argentina. PNAS 20 104 (30): 12398-12403.

DICKISON M. R. 2007: The Allometry of Giant Flightless Birds. Department of Biology, Duke University, Dissertation.

DYKE G. J., G. W. KAISER 2010: Cracking a Developmental Constraint: Egg Size and Bird Evolution. Records of the Australian Museum 62: 207–216.

GILL B. J. 2007: Eggshell characteristics of moa eggs (*Aves: Dinornithiformes*). Journal of the Royal Society of New Zealand 37:4, 139-150.

GILL B. J. 2006: A Catalogue of Moa Eggs (*Aves: Dinornithiformes*). Rec. Auckland Mus. 43: 55–80.

GRELLET-TINNER G., L. E. FIORELLI 2010: A new Argentinean nesting site showing neosauropod dinosaur reproduction in a Cretaceous hydrothermal environment. Nat. Commun. 1:32

GRELLET-TINNER G. ET AL. 2016: Is the "Genyornis" egg of a mihirung or another extinct bird from the Australian dreamtime? Quaternary Science Reviews 133: 147-164.

HANDLEY, W.D. ET AL. 2016: Sexual dimorphism in the late Miocene mihirung *Dromornis stirtoni* (*Aves*: *Dromornithidae*) from the Alcoota Local Fauna of central Australia. Journal of Vertebrate Paleontology 36(5): e1180298 (21 pages).

KRÖSCHE O. 2006: Die Moa-Strausse: Neuseelands ausgestorbene Riesenvögel. Taschenbuch Westarp; 2nd edition, reprint from 1963.

MURRAY P. F., P.VICKERS-RICH. 2004: Magnificent Mihirungs. The Colossal Flightless Birds of the Australian Dreamtime. Indiana University Press, Bloomington, Indiana. ISBN 0253342821.

NGUYEN J. M. T. ET AL. 2010: New Material of *Barawertornis tedfordi*, a Dromornithid Bird from the Oligo-Miocene of Australia, and its Phylogenetic Implications. Records of the Australian Museum (2010) Vol. 62: 45–60.

PALMQVIST P. S., F. VIZCAÍNO 2003: Ecological and reproductive constraints of body size in the gigantic *Argentavis magnificens* (*Aves*, *Theratornithidae*) from the Miocene of Argentina. AMEGHINIANA (Rev. Asoc. Paleontol. Argent.) 40 (3): 379-385.

RAHN H., ET AL. 1975: Relation of Avian Egg Weight to Body Weight. The Auk 92: 750-765.

RICH P. V. 1979: The *Dromornithidae*, an extinct family of large ground birds endemic to Australia.

Bureau of National Resources, Geology and Geophysics, Bulletin 184.

SCHLÄPFER K. 2015: *Aepyornis* eggs: History, characteristics and market. downloaded from http://www.natureier.ch.

SCHÖNWETTER M. 1960-1992: Handbuch der Oologie. 4 vol., Akademie Verlag, Berlin.

SCHÖNWETTER M. 1985: Handbuch der Oologie. Vol 4: 34-35, Akademie Verlag, Berlin.

SCHÖNWETTER M. 1960: Handbuch der Oologie. Vol 1: 33, Akademie Verlag, Berlin.

WORTHY T. H. ET AL 2017: The evolution of giant flightless birds and novel phylogenetic relationships for extinct fowl (*Aves, Galloanseres*). R. Soc. Open Sci. 4: 170975, Data Supplement SI 8.

WORTHY T. H., R. N. HOLDAWAY 2002: The Lost World of the Moa: Prehistoric Life of New Zealand (Life of the Past). Indiana University Press Bloomington and Indianapolis. ISBN 0-253-34034-9.

# 2. The egg of the Great Elephantbird (*Aepyornis maximus*)

---

*One can safely say that the eggs of the Great Elephantbird are more famous than the bird itself. This is due to the fact that considerably more eggs exist than other remains of the bird. In addition, the eggs are the biggest that an animal has ever laid, whereas the Great Elephantbird itself was (probably) not the largest bird of all time.*

**Taxonomy**

Fossil evidence indicates that several species of elephantbirds ranging from 90 cm to 3 metres in size had inhabited Madagascar, but most had died out long before our time. The taxonomy of elephantbirds is still subject of debate, in particular as to the actual number of species involved. A widely accepted consensus is that seven or eight species once occurred on Madagascar, four in the genus *Aepyornis* and three or four in *Mullerornis.* However, for the genus *Aepyornis* numerous authors tend to assume that there is just one species, the Great Elephantbird (*Aepyornis maximus*). This species has most probably survived until 1649. The species of the genus *Mullerornis* represent the smaller elephant birds which are known only from subfossil remains and from which no egg has been preserved. A bone belonging to *Mullerornis* has been radiocarbon dated to about 1260 before our era, suggesting that the bird was still extant 3300 years ago. As all currently existing eggs originate from the genus *Aepyornis,* and as it is likely that all eggs belong to one species, they are simply called *Aepyornis* eggs.

**The history of the *Aepyornis* eggs**

In 1850 the captain of a French merchant ship stayed in Madagascar and discovered in the house of a villager a drinking vessel, which – on closer inspection – turned out to be the shell of a large egg whose upper part was removed.

He asked the villagers whether they can also provide intact eggs and, as a result, he obtained three pieces which he brought to Paris. Unfortunately, one of the eggs broke to pieces. The eggs were given to the French zoologist I. Geoffroy Saint-Hilaire who assigned them to a new species, which he called *Aepyornis maximus*. (The name *Aepyornis* is derived from the ancient Greek and means as much as "tall bird"). 1851, he presented these eggs to the Academy of Sciences in Paris. Four years later, he was able to show the next two eggs. Museums became soon aware that these eggs are an interesting collector's item, with the consequence that the number of eggs coming to Europe was rapidly growing. As early as in 1901, a first list of eggs was published comprising 33 entries, 30 of which were described by their dimensions. Other egg lists were published in 1931, 1957, 1960 and in 2003. Not the most comprehensive but the most detailed list appeared in 1960 in the *Handbuch für Oologie* Vol. 1, by MAX SCHÖNWETTER (1960-1992). Apart from the dimensions of the eggs this list includes the eggshell weight and the eggshell thickness.

*Figure 5: Eggs in a size comparison:*
*Left: Great Elephantbird (Aeypornis maximus)*
*Center: Common Ostrich*
*Right: domestic chicken*

It can be estimated that, today, about 80 *Aepyornis* eggs are owned by museums and institutional collections and more than 25 eggs are privately owned. A list of all *Aepyornis* eggs classified by countries (see table 4) shows a total number of 78. This list only considers the institutional owners. It is possible that further eggs are in countries not listed here, as for instance in China or in Japan. Table 4 not only covers intact eggs, but also eggs that are partly broken or have missing shell fragments, and even eggs that are pieced together from their eggshell fragments. Not included in table 4 are eggs which are reconstructed from shell fragments of different eggs. The number of such eggs has increased in the last years and to list them is beyond the scope of this survey.

*Table 4: Aepyornis eggs in museums and in institutional collections (without privately owned eggs and eggs sold at auctions)*

| Country | Number |
|---|---|
| Australia | 3 |
| Germany | 9 |
| United Kingdom | 10 |
| Finland | 1 |
| France | 14 |
| Greece | 1 |
| Netherlands | 2 |
| India | 1 |
| Ireland | 1 |
| Italy | 1 |
| Canada | 1 |
| New Zealand | 1 |
| Austria | 1 |
| Poland | 2 |
| Russia | 1 |
| Switzerland | 8 |
| Slovakia | 1 |
| Hungary | 1 |
| USA | 19 |

## Characteristics of *Aepyornis* eggs

Table 5 shows a listing of 63 eggs whose dimensions are known from publications or from other sources. Using the values for the length and the width, the author has calculated the volume and the weight of the eggs. The volume of *Aepyornis* eggs can be calculated almost exactly from the length and width, because the eggs have a nearly ideal elliptical form. For the calculation of the volume $V$ from the length $L$ and the width $B$, the following formula can be used:

$$V = 0.5236 \times L \times B^2$$

*Table 5: List of 63 Aepyornis eggs*

|  | Measured values | | | Calculated values | |
|---|---|---|---|---|---|
|  | Length mm | Width mm | Shell weight g | Volume ml | Mass g |
| Toulouse FRA | 264 | 194 | 1233 | 5202 | 5983 |
| Bonn GER | 280 | 199 | 1116 | 5806 | 6677 |
| Perth AUS | 276 | 207 |  | 6192 | 7121 |
| Heritage Auctions 2014 | 297 | 203 |  | 6408 | 7370 |
| Dublin IRL | 270 | 213 |  | 6414 | 7376 |
| Solothurn SUI | 295 | 206 | 1446 | 6555 | 7538 |
| London GBR | 280 | 213 | 2300 | 6651 | 7649 |
| St. Omer FRA | 280 | 213 | 1500 | 6651 | 7649 |
| Tring GBR | 285 | 213 | 1560 | 6770 | 7786 |
| Bern SUI | 280 | 216 | 1735 | 6840 | 7866 |
| Dresden GER | 285 | 215 | 1580 | 6898 | 7933 |
| Tring GBR | 285 | 217 | 1645 | 7027 | 8081 |
| Sens FRA | 305 | 210 |  | 7043 | 8099 |
| Berlin GER | 296 | 215 | 1490 | 7164 | 8239 |
| Bonn GER | 297 | 215 | 1451 | 7188 | 8267 |
| Camarillo USA | 290 | 218 | 1790 | 7216 | 8299 |
| Private | 293 | 217 |  | 7224 | 8308 |
| Athen GRE | 298 | 217 | 1380 | 7347 | 8450 |
| Lyon FRA | 299 | 217 |  | 7372 | 8478 |
| Camarillo USA | 305 | 215 | 1610 | 7382 | 8489 |
| Leiden NED | 314 | 212 | 1610 | 7389 | 8498 |
| Basel SUI | 296 | 220 | 1615 | 7501 | 8626 |
| Freiburg SUI | 300 | 220 | 1739 | 7603 | 8743 |

| | Measured values | | | Calculated values | |
|---|---|---|---|---|---|
| | Length mm | Width mm | Shell weight g | Volume ml | Mass g |
| Bologna ITA | 300 | 220 | | 7603 | 8743 |
| Tring GBR | 297 | 222 | 1645 | 7664 | 8814 |
| Paris FRA | 310 | 220 | | 7856 | 9035 |
| Camarillo USA | 310 | 220 | 1555 | 7856 | 9035 |
| Heritage Auctions 2012 | 311 | 220 | | 7881 | 9064 |
| Schönenwerd SUI | 299 | 225 | 1739 | 7926 | 9115 |
| Frankfurt GER | 298 | 227 | 1652 | 8040 | 9246 |
| Camarillo USA | 305 | 225 | 1250 | 8085 | 9297 |
| Quebec CAN | 332 | 217 | 1580 | 8186 | 9414 |
| Paris FRA | 300 | 229 | | 8237 | 9473 |
| Private | 310 | 226 | | 8290 | 9534 |
| Stuttgart GER | 300 | 230 | | 8310 | 9556 |
| Wien AUT | 307 | 228 | | 8356 | 9610 |
| Christie's 2013 | 305 | 229 | | 8375 | 9631 |
| Dresden GER | 305 | 229 | 1850 | 8375 | 9631 |
| Hildesheim | 306 | 231 | 1665 | 8550 | 9832 |
| Heritage Auctions 2011 | 317 | 227 | | 8553 | 9836 |
| Camarillo USA | 315 | 228 | 1655 | 8574 | 9860 |
| Budapest HUN | 292 | 237 | | 8588 | 9876 |
| Private | 325 | 225 | | 8615 | 9907 |
| St. Omer FRA | 309 | 232 | 1800 | 8708 | 10015 |
| Private | 305 | 234 | | 8744 | 10056 |
| Paris FRA | 320 | 230 | | 8864 | 10193 |
| Paris FRA | 340 | 225 | 2000 | 9012 | 10364 |
| Warmbrunn POL | 315 | 234 | 2360 | 9031 | 10386 |
| Perth AUS | 317 | 234 | | 9088 | 10452 |
| Private | 311 | 238 | | 9224 | 10607 |
| Christie's 2009 | 310 | 239 | | 9272 | 10662 |
| Tring GBR | 316 | 237 | 1935 | 9294 | 10688 |
| Private | 310 | 240 | 2715 | 9349 | 10752 |
| Private | 330 | 233 | | 9380 | 10788 |
| Tring GBR | 314 | 242 | 2025 | 9629 | 11073 |
| Camarillo USA | 318 | 242 | 1710 | 9751 | 11214 |
| Private | 315 | 244 | | 9820 | 11292 |
| Helsinki FIN | 337 | 236 | | 9828 | 11302 |
| Paris FRA | 334 | 238 | | 9906 | 11392 |

|  | Measured values | | | Calculated values | |
|---|---|---|---|---|---|
|  | Length mm | Width mm | Shell weight g | Volume ml | Mass g |
| Bhubaneswar IND | 330 | 240 |  | 9953 | 11445 |
| Christie's 2008 | 330 | 240 |  | 9953 | 11445 |
| Denver USA | 330 | 243 |  | 10203 | 11733 |
| London GBR | 340 | 245 | 3346 | 10686 | 12289 |
| **Mean value** | **305.5** | **224.5** |  | **8118** | **9336** |

To calculate the egg weight $W$, the specific weight is required which, however, depends on the weight of the eggshell. As an average value 1.15 can be used. The formula is then:
$$W = 1.15 \times V$$
The calculated weight values of the present 63 eggs range from 6.0 kg to 12.3 kg.

To summarize the calculations of the author, an average *Aepyornis* egg has the following characteristics:
- Length: 306 mm
- Width: 225 mm
- Volume: 8.12 litres
- Egg weight: 9.34 kg
- Eggshell weight: 1.64 kg
- Eggshell thickness: 3.30 mm
- Specific weight (of the full egg): 1.15

Just to remind: An average chicken egg weighs 60 g, and an ostrich egg – the biggest egg which is laid by an extant bird – 1.6 kg. This permits the following comparison: The weight of an *Aepyornis* egg corresponds to nearly six ostrich eggs and to about 155 chicken eggs. It is clear that an egg with a capacity of 155 chicken eggs was a welcome food source for the local population of Madagascar, so that the excessive hunt after these eggs might be one of the reasons, why the elephantbirds became extinct.

**The *Aepyornis* eggs as article of trade**
There are not only the eggs stored in museums, but there is also a veritable market for collectors or institutions who want to acquire such an egg (or a replica). The eggs offered for sale can be divided into the following categories:
- Completely intact eggs: These are not blown out or have a blowhole of a few centimetres of diameter. Such eggs are offered by auction houses (e.g. Christie's or Sotheby) where they fetch very high prices (examples see below).
- Eggs with cracks or missing shell fragments or with inserted fragments, (if they origin from the same egg).
- Eggs which are composed from shell fragments of different eggs: If it is an almost seamless reconstruction, such eggs are also offered at auctions under the term "reconstructed eggs". Eggs with visible adhesive joints are sold by fossil retailers and on Internet platforms for prices of more than 1,000 US$.
- Replica eggs made from plaster with glued-in eggshell fragments: Eggs of this kind are produced in Madagascar and sold on local markets or abroad. Genuine eggshell fragments can still be found on some beaches in the south of Madagascar. However, the exportation of such fragments is forbidden for tourists.
- Replica eggs completely made from plastics (polyurethane resin) and hand-finished to simulate the shell structure: Such copies look deceptively real and are for sale for less than 50 US$.

It is clear that museums were always anxious to acquire genuine and intact *Aepyornis* eggs for their collections. However, while the eggs of extant birds have no sales prices, *Aepyornis* eggs had always to be acquired by purchase. Therefore, it might be of interest to see how the prices in this "market" developed.

*Figure 6: Reconstructed Aepyornis eggs:*
*Left: Carefully made reconstruction from shell fragments of different eggs.*
*Right: Reconstruction with conspicuous adhesive joints.*

Around 1900, *Aepyornis* eggs were traded in the USA and in Great Britain for 200 to 1,100 US$ (today about 5,000 to 27,000 US$). After 2000, over 25 *Aepyornis* eggs were offered for sale at auctions. Here some prize examples for immaculate eggs:

| Year | Auction house | Price US$ |
| --- | --- | --- |
| 2004 | Binhams | 41,125 |
| 2007 | Christie's | 97,672 |
| 2008 | Christie's | 134,173 |
| 2008 | Christie's | 57,730 |
| 2009 | Christie's | 68,900 |
| 2012 | Sotheby | 47,512 |
| 2013 | Christie's | 101,813 |
| 2014 | Christie's | 205,555 |

As this small list shows, typical prices for intact eggs are nowadays above 50,000 US$. But the enormous price differences and in particular the maximum price of more than

200,000 US$ are difficult to explain. Maybe the most expensive egg was simply at the right time for sale, when several bidders wanted to buy this egg at any price. In contrast to intact eggs, reconstructed eggs are offered only seldom at auctions. But if so, they can achieve prices up to 20,000 US$. Reconstructed eggs looking less immaculate are often found on Internet platforms, sometimes for prices less than 5,000 US$.

## References

BRADBURY W. C. 1919: Some notes on the egg of *Aepyornis maximus.* Condor 21: 97-101.

CAUDEREY H. 1931: Etude sur l'*Aepyornis.* L'Oiseaux et la Revue Française d'Ornithologie 1: 624-644.

HENRICI P. 1957: *Aepyornis*-Eier. Mitteilungen der Naturforschenden Gesellschaft in Bern 14: 135-139.

LONG J. A. ET AL. 1998: The Cervantes egg: an early Malagasy tourist to Australia. Records of the Western Australian Museum 19: 39-46.

MLIKOVSKY J. 2003: Eggs of the extinct aepyornithids (*Aves: Aepyornithidae*) of Madagaskar: size and taxonomic identity. Sylvia 39: 133-138.

SCHÖNWETTER M. 1960-1992: *Aepyornithiformes.* Vol. 1: 31-34.

# 3. The eggs of the tinamous

---

*There are many bird species laying brightly colored eggs. But the eggs of the tinamous are particularly colourful. In addition, they have a glossy surface, as if they were painted. They give the impression that this conspicuous coloration is intended. Many researchers have tried to explain this phenomenon, but not in a satisfactory way.*

**Taxonomy**
The tinamou family (*Tinamidae*) consists of 47 species and 125 subspecies in nine genera. This classification is based on the *IOC World Bird List v 7.3, 2017*).

*Table 6: Genera, species and subspecies of the family of Tinamidae*

| Genus | Species | Subspecies |
|---|---|---|
| *Crypturellus* | 21 | 55 |
| *Eudromia* | 2 | 12 |
| *Nothocercus* | 3 | 7 |
| *Nothoprocta* | 6 | 17 |
| *Nothura* | 5 | 13 |
| *Rhynchotus* | 2 | 3 |
| *Taoniscus* | 1 | 0 |
| *Tinamotis* | 2 | 0 |
| *Tinamus* | 5 | 18 |
| **Total** | **47** | **125** |

Two other international checklists (*BirdLife International Checklist of the Birds of the World, Version 9,* and the *Handbook of the Birds of the World Alive*) list 48 species. In these checklists, the additional species is *Crypturellus occidentalis*. This species is listed in the *IOC World Bird List v. 7.3* as subspecies *Crypturellus cinnamomeus occidentalis*. The following table 7 shows the 47 species of the *Tinamidae* family.

*Table 7: Names of the 47 tinamou species*

| Common name | Scientific name |
| --- | --- |
| Black-capped Tinamou | *Crypturellus atrocapillus* |
| Bartlett's Tinamou | *Crypturellus bartletti* |
| Berlepsch's Tinamou | *Crypturellus berlepschi* |
| Slaty-breasted Tinamou | *Crypturellus boucardi* |
| Rusty Tinamou | *Crypturellus brevirostris* |
| Barred Tinamou | *Crypturellus casiquiare* |
| Cinereous Tinamou | *Crypturellus cinereus* |
| Eastern Thicket Tinamou | *Crypturellus cinnamomeus* |
| Grey-legged Tinamou | *Crypturellus duidae* |
| Red-legged Tinamou | *Crypturellus erythropus* |
| Choco Tinamou | *Crypturellus kerriae* |
| Yellow-legged Tinamou | *Crypturellus noctivagus* |
| Brown Tinamou | *Crypturellus obsoletus* |
| Small-billed Tinamou | *Crypturellus parvirostris* |
| Tepui Tinamou | *Crypturellus ptaritepui* |
| Little Tinamou | *Crypturellus soui* |
| Brazilian Tinamou | *Crypturellus strigulosus* |
| Tataupa Tinamou | *Crypturellus tataupa* |
| Pale-browed Tinamou | *Crypturellus transfasciatus* |
| Undulated Tinamou | *Crypturellus undulatus* |
| Variegated Tinamou | *Crypturellus variegatus* |
| Elegant Crested Tinamou | *Eudromia elegans* |
| Quebracho Crested Tinamou | *Eudromia formosa* |
| Highland Tinamou | *Nothocercus bonapartei* |
| Tawny-breasted Tinamou | *Nothocercus julius* |
| Hooded Tinamou | *Nothocercus nigrocapillus* |
| Brushland Tinamou | *Nothoprocta cinerascens* |
| Curve-billed Tinamou | *Nothoprocta curvirostris* |
| Ornate Tinamou | *Nothoprocta ornata* |
| Andean Tinamou | *Nothoprocta pentlandii* |
| Chilean Tinamou | *Nothoprocta perdicaria* |
| Taczanowski's Tinamou | *Nothoprocta taczanowskii* |
| White-bellied Nothura | *Nothura boraquira* |
| Chaco Nothura | *Nothura chacoensis* |
| Darwin's Nothura | *Nothura darwinii* |
| Spotted Nothura | *Nothura maculosa* |
| Lesser Nothura | *Nothura minor* |
| Huayco Tinamou | *Rhynchotus maculicollis* |
| Red-winged Tinamou | *Rhynchotus rufescens* |

| Dwarf Tinamou | *Taoniscus nanus* |
| --- | --- |
| Patagonian Tinamou | *Tinamotis ingoufi* |
| Puna Tinamou | *Tinamotis pentlandii* |
| White-throated Tinamou | *Tinamus guttatus* |
| Great Tinamou | *Tinamus major* |
| Black Tinamou | *Tinamus osgoodi* |
| Solitary Tinamou | *Tinamus solitarius* |
| Grey Tinamou | *Tinamus tao* |

## The colors of the tinamou eggs

To describe the colors of tinamou eggs, an obvious approach is to measure eggs from museum collections. However, as eggshell pigments are natural dyes, they have a relatively low resistance to light and storage. In nature this is not relevant, because the function of the eggshell color becomes obsolete after the chick has hatched. For the egg collectors and museums, however, the low color fastness is a serious problem.

*Figure 7: The Elegant Crested Tinamou with its bright green eggs*
*(Exhibit in Naturmuseum Senckenberg, Frankfurt am Main)*

Despite proper storage, many museum eggs do not show the color that the eggshell had when the egg was laid. Some freshly laid eggs lose their coloration often in the first days after being laid. An example for this are the tinamou eggs of the genus *Crypturellus,* which have a purple coloration when freshly laid and tend to look brownish after a short time. But not all color shades tend equally to discoloration. A very popular tinamou egg color is the vivid green of the *Eudromia elegans* which appears even after a longer storage period almost unaffected. This is due to the fact, that the green coloration is based on a pigment containing zinc (zinc biliverdin), and this metal component contributes to a higher stability of the coloration.

In order to measure the color of freshly laid eggs, photos in the Internet are well suited. The author of this study was able to collect 60 pictures of tinamou nests from 29 species. A reliable method to measure the color is using a *Color Picker* application. This allows to read the RGB values which can then be converted to visually perceived color coordinates. Whether the eggshell colors on these pictures are correctly rendered, depends on the illumination (daylight or sunlight) and the brightness level. Moreover, the color of the surrounding area has an influence on the egg appearance. Therefore, the aim of these measurements cannot be to attribute a particular color to a species, but to find the range in which the egg colors of the tinamous are typically located.

Table 10 shows the color values of the eggs of 32 tinamou species. For 29 species, the color has been measured from pictures of eggs found in ground nests. For three species, only eggshells from collections were available for color measurements. Broadly speaking, the following color shades can be distinguished:
- Purple and violet eggs are typical for the genus *Crypturellus.*
- Greenish-blue or bluish-green eggs are typical for the genera *Tinamus* and *Nothocercus.*
- Green and yellow-green eggs are typical for the species *Eudromia elegans, Eudromia formosa* and *Tinamotis pentlandii.*
- Brown eggs can be found for some species of the genera *Nothura* and *Nothoprocta.*

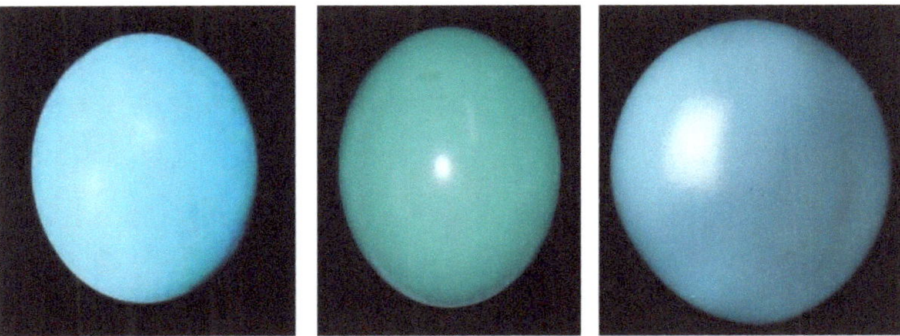

*Figure 8: Eggs of 15 of the 47 tinamou species*
*(For better comparability the eggs are shown in approximately the same size.)*

*In table 8 the eggs are assigned to the species names. The order in the table corresponds to the order of the pictures, starting from top left to bottom right.*

*Table 8: Tinamou species whose eggs are shown in figure 8*

| | |
|---|---|
| *Crypturellus noctivagus* | Yellow-legged Tinamou |
| *Crypturellus obsoletus* | Brown Tinamou |
| *Crypturellus parvirostris* | Small-billed Tinamou |
| *Crypturellus transfasciatus* | Pale-browed Tinamou |
| *Crypturellus variegatus* | Variegated Tinamou |
| *Eudromia elegans* | Elegant Crested Tinamou |
| *Nothoprocta curvirostris* | Curve-billed Tinamou |
| *Nothoprocta pentlandii* | Andean Tinamou |
| *Nothoprocta perdicaria* | Chilean Tinamou |
| *Nothura boraquira* | White-bellied Tinamou |
| *Rhynchotus rufescens* | Red-winged Tinamou |
| *Tinamotis pentlandii* | Puna Tinamou |
| *Tinamus major* | Great Tinamou |
| *Tinamus guttatus* | White-throated Tinamou |
| *Tinamus osgoodi* | Black Tinamou |

The brown color, however, can also be the result of a discoloration occurring after a certain period of storage. As mentioned above, this may occur with eggs of the genus *Cryp-*

*turellus* which are purple or violet immediately after oviposition. The color shown on the next pages for the *Crypturellus cinnamomeus* could be an example, as this egg comes from a museum collection.

As the author of this study has additionally measured tinamou eggs in egg collections, a comparison can be made between freshly laid eggs and eggs from collections. This shows how the eggshell colors change after a certain period of time.

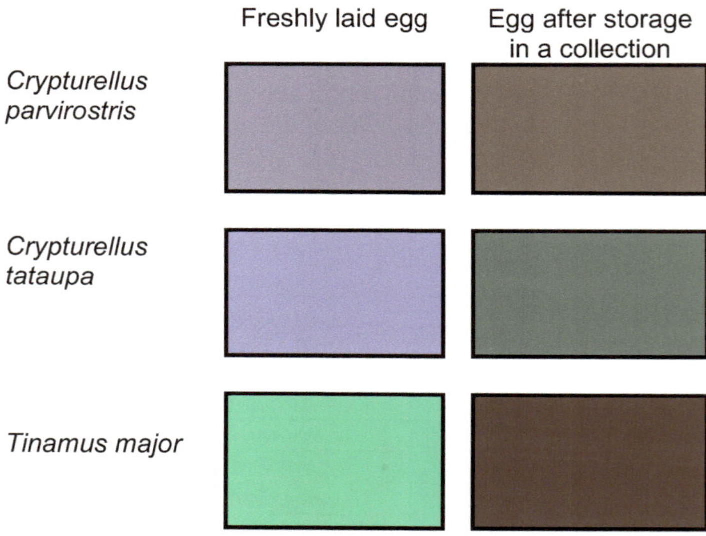


*Figure 9: Coloration of freshly laid eggs compare to eggs stored in a collection*

## How egg predators perceive colors

Eggs of ground nesting birds that lack camouflage or even have conspicuous colors are exceptional. However, what we perceive as camouflaged or conspicuous, is based on the human color vision system. In contrast, most nest predators such as mammals, birds and reptiles see colors differently than humans.

In the human visual system, there are three color receptors and, as a consequence, any color can be defined by three attributes, for instance hue, saturation and brightness. This is called trichromatic color vision or trichromacy. In the world of animals, color vision systems can (apart from trichromatic) be monochromatic, dichromatic, tetrachromatic and even pentachromatic, where the prefix mono-, di-, tri-, tetra- and penta- refer to the number of available color receptors. Monochromatic and dichromatic vision also occur in the human color vision, if one or two color receptors are defective. Therefore, monochromacy, dichromacy and trichromacy are well investigated. The number of color receptors has a decisive influence of the number of perceived colors. Under average illumination conditions one color receptor can discriminate about 50 thresholds. A dichromat (an animal with dichromatic color vision) can therefore perceive 50 × 50 = 2,500 colors, a trichromat 125,000 colors, a tetrachromat 6,250,000 colors and a pentachromat 312,500,000 colors.

Most mammals are dichromats, meaning that they have only two types of color receptors. When considering the mammalian families representing the most important avian nests predators, there is variation in the sensitivity of their color receptors. But the restricted perceivable color gamut is common to all dichromats. The comparison below clearly shows that dichromats perceive an egg color as far less conspicuous then humans do.

*Figure 10: Egg of the Crypturellus variegatus on a forest floor: On the right is simulated, how this egg appears to most of the mammalian dichromats.*

Primates are also common nest predators. However their visual system can be, depending on the family and species, either trichromatic or dichromatic.

*Table 9: Color vision as a function of the number of color receptors*

| Color vision | Color receptors | Receptor carriers |
|---|---|---|
| Monochromacy | 1 | marine mammals |
| Dichromacy | 2 | most terrestrial non-primate mammals |
| Trichromacy | 3 | humans, most primates, some insects (such as honeybees) |
| Tetrachromacy | 4 | most reptiles, amphibians, birds and insects |
| Pentachromacy | 5 | some insects (specific species of butterflies), some birds (pigeons for instance) |

Other than mammals, birds possess four color receptors and have tetrachromatic vision. The fourth receptor is sensitive to UV light, meaning that birds see wavelengths which are invisible to humans.

## The size of tinamou eggs

The author was able to collect eggshell data (length, width, egg mass) from 36 tinamou species (see table 11). The source for these data is (with three exceptions) the *Handbuch der Oologie*, (SCHÖNWETTER M. 1960-1992, Vol. 1: 41-46). Where SCHÖNWETTER has listed data for different subspecies, those of the subspecies with the largest eggs are used. The egg mass values range from 12 g (*Taoniscus nanus*) to 105 g (*Nothocercus bonapartei*). Compared with a chicken egg of 60 g, the eggs of 29 tinamou species are smaller.

*Table 10: Color values of tinamou eggs (32 species)*

*The values H (hue), L (luminance) und C (chroma) are the coordinates of the CIELAB color space. RGB are the coordinates of the sRGB color space.*

*N/C: egg from a nest (N) or a collection (C)*

| Species | H | L | C | R | G | B | N/C |
|---|---|---|---|---|---|---|---|
| *Crypturellus bartletti* | 294 | 78 | 13 | 193 | 191 | 215 | N |
| *Crypturellus cinerus* | 29 | 73 | 37 | 244 | 155 | 147 | N |
| *Crypturellus erythropus* | 292 | 74 | 21 | 180 | 180 | 218 | N |
| *Crypturellus obsoletus* | 358 | 80 | 28 | 249 | 181 | 202 | N |
| *Crypturellus tataupa* | 303 | 70 | 24 | 178 | 165 | 208 | N |
| *Crypturellus cinnamomeus* | 63 | 49 | 18 | 139 | 110 | 89 | C |
| *Crypturellus noctivagus* | 179 | 69 | 39 | 63 | 187 | 166 | N |
| *Crypturellus parvirostris* | 313 | 68 | 15 | 176 | 161 | 186 | N |
| *Crypturellus soui* | 309 | 69 | 21 | 180 | 163 | 199 | N |
| *Crypturellus transfasciatus* | 335 | 77 | 8 | 201 | 185 | 196 | N |
| *Crypturellus undulatus* | 332 | 84 | 13 | 228 | 205 | 223 | N |
| *Crypturellus variegatus* | 353 | 68 | 40 | 230 | 138 | 177 | N |
| *Eudromia elegans* | 111 | 68 | 66 | 156 | 176 | 43 | N |
| *Eudromia formosa* | 111 | 61 | 54 | 141 | 156 | 53 | N |
| *Nothocercus bonapartei* | 208 | 77 | 35 | 81 | 207 | 219 | N |
| *Nothocercus nigrocapillus* | 196 | 83 | 46 | 1 | 231 | 231 | N |
| *Nothoprocta cinerascens* | 88 | 51 | 15 | 133 | 121 | 97 | N |

| Species | H | L | C | R | G | B | N/C |
| --- | --- | --- | --- | --- | --- | --- | --- |
| *Nothoprocta curvirostris* | 1 | 76 | 16 | 217 | 177 | 187 | N |
| *Nothoprocta ornata* | 6 | 73 | 24 | 224 | 164 | 176 | N |
| *Nothoprocta pentlandii* | 20 | 55 | 18 | 162 | 120 | 121 | N |
| *Nothoprocta perdicaria* | 301 | 52 | 22 | 127 | 118 | 155 | N |
| *Nothura boraquira* | 313 | 55 | 20 | 143 | 124 | 156 | N |
| *Nothura darwinii* | 70 | 78 | 26 | 142 | 108 | 73 | C |
| *Nothura maculosa* | 325 | 48 | 17 | 130 | 106 | 130 | N |
| *Nothura minor* | 63 | 55 | 20 | 158 | 125 | 101 | C |
| *Rhynchotus rufescens* | 8 | 68 | 19 | 202 | 155 | 163 | N |
| *Tinamotis pentlandii* | 107 | 84 | 56 | 211 | 215 | 104 | N |
| *Tinamus guttatus* | 197 | 84 | 46 | 18 | 232 | 233 | N |
| *Tinamus major* | 166 | 78 | 44 | 97 | 214 | 172 | N |
| *Tinamus osgoodi* | 218 | 63 | 18 | 110 | 162 | 173 | C |
| *Tinamus solitarius* | 184 | 84 | 43 | 83 | 230 | 212 | N |
| *Tinamus tao* | 185 | 74 | 32 | 98 | 198 | 186 | N |

*Table 11: Size of 36 tinamou eggs*

| Species | Egg length mm | Egg width mm | Egg mass g |
|---|---|---|---|
| *Crypturellus bartletti* | 54 | 37 | 40 |
| *Crypturellus berlepschi* | 44 | 39 | 35 |
| *Crypturellus boucardi* | 42 | 32 | 23 |
| *Crypturellus cinerus* | 48 | 39 | 40 |
| *Crypturellus cinnamomeus* | 46 | 39 | 37 |
| *Crypturellus erythropus* | 54 | 41 | 48 |
| *Crypturellus noctivagus* | 52 | 41 | 47 |
| *Crypturellus obsoletus* | 53 | 37 | 41 |
| *Crypturellus parvirostris* | 39 | 28 | 17 |
| *Crypturellus soui* | 41 | 32 | 24 |
| *Crypturellus strigulosus* | 51 | 37 | 37 |
| *Crypturellus tataupa* | 41 | 30 | 19 |
| *Crypturellus transfasciatus* | 51 | 40 | 44 |
| *Crypturellus undulatus* | 54 | 40 | 45 |
| *Crypturellus variegatus* | 52 | 37 | 37 |
| *Eudromia elegans* | 56 | 41 | 51 |
| *Nothocercus bonapartei* | 74 | 51 | 105 |
| *Nothocercus nigrocapillus* | 69 | 47 | 89 |
| *Nothoprocta cinerascens* | 48 | 37 | 34 |
| *Nothoprocta curvirostris* | 54 | 37 | 40 |
| *Nothoprocta ornata* | 56 | 38 | 43 |
| *Nothoprocta perdicaria* | 50 | 36 | 34 |
| *Nothoprocta pentlandii* | 51 | 35 | 34 |
| *Nothura boraquira* | 46 | 33 | 27 |
| *Nothura darwinii* | 45 | 32 | 23 |
| *Nothura maculosa* | 44 | 32 | 24 |
| *Nothura minor* | 37 | 28 | 15 |
| *Rhynchotus rufescens* | 60 | 44 | 59 |
| *Taoniscus nanus* | 35 | 26 | 12 |
| *Tinamotis ingoufi* | 57 | 41 | 51 |
| *Tinamotis pentlandii* | 54 | 38 | 43 |
| *Tinamus guttatus* | 55 | 46 | 63 |
| *Tinamus major* | 59 | 48 | 75 |
| *Tinamus osgoodi* | 54 | 49 | 70 |
| *Tinamus solitarius* | 67 | 48 | 83 |
| *Tinamus tao* | 65 | 54 | 103 |

# 4. The egg of the Common Murre

*The eggs of the Common Murre are fascinating, because they have a very distinctive shape and unique individual patterns. Many scientists have tried to explain the pear like shape of these eggs. It was long assumed that the shape allowed the egg to roll in an arc to avoid falling off the cliff edge where the birds breed. Recent publications contradict this popular theory (BIRKHEAD 2017b).*

## Taxonomy
The "official" name of this species (*Uria aalge*) is Common Murre (GILL 2018). Common Guillemot is the name still used for this species in the UK. The Common Murre belongs to the family of auks (*Alcidae*), which consists of 11 genera, 25 species and 27 subspecies (*IOC Bird List v 8.1, 2018*).

## The egg of the Common Murre
An average Common Murre egg has the following characteristics (SCHÖNWETTER 1960-1992):
- Length: 81 mm
- Width: 50 mm
- Volume: 98 ml
- Weight: 107 g
- Eggshell weight: 12.1 g

The above data are subject to a considerable variation, e.g. the egg weight can vary between 70 g and 165 g.

The outstanding feature of these eggs is their unusual shape. It can be described as pear-shaped or conical or gyroscopic. To describe this shape in numerical terms, mathematical equations can be used. A simpler way of describing this egg shape is to determine how far the maximum width of the egg deviates from the middle of the longitudinal axis (see figure 11). The ratio of the values *a* and *b* can be referred to as asymmetry:

*Asymmetry = a/b*

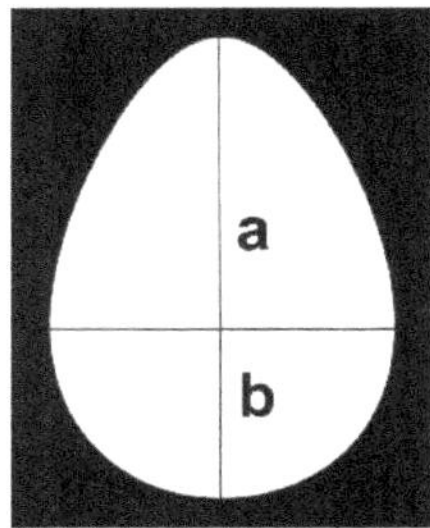

*Figure 11: Values a and b used to calculate the asymmetry*

In some publications (BIRKHEAD 2017a) the values *a* and *b* are used to calculate a parameter referred to as pointedness:
*Pointedness = a/(a+b)*

In addition, the ratio of egg length *L* to egg width *B* (axial ratio) can be used to determine how far the egg is stretched, i.e. elliptical.
*Ellipticity = L/B*

Typical values for the asymmetry and the ellipticity of the Common Murre eggs compared to a chicken egg are:

| Egg | Asymmetry | Ellipticity |
|---|---|---|
| Common Murre | 1.78 | 1.62 |
| Domestic chicken | 1.20 | 1.37 |

*Figure 12: A Common Murre egg (right) compared to a chicken egg*

Moreover, the Common Murre eggs show great variation in color and markings. The coloration can be blue, greenish, brownish and at times white. The eggs are marked with variable amounts of dark streaks or blotches.

*Figure 13: The individual patterns of Common Murre eggs*

As Common Murre eggs were admired for their shape and color, they were popular collector's items. In the days when egg collecting was not prohibited by law, cliff climbers, so called "climmers", collected the eggs from the cliff legdes. At a time when three British pounds were a weekly wage for farm worker, selling eggs was an important source of additional income. The commoner egg shapes and colors went for a few pennies. The rarest guillemot eggs were those of a port-wine or blood red color. Such unusually coloured eggs sold for one British pound (BIRKHEAD 2018).

## References

BIRKHEAD T. R. ET AL. 2017a: The Point of a Guillemot's Egg. Ibis 159: 255-265.

BIRKHEAD T. R. ET AL. 2017b: Egg shape in the Common Guillemot *Uria aalge* and Brunnich's Guillemot *U. lomvia*: not a rolling matter? J Ornithol 158: 679-685.

BIRKHEAD T. 2018: Red Eggs. downloaded from https://amornithhistory.org/2018/04/30/red-eggs

GILL, F., D. DONSKER (Eds) 2018: IOC World Bird List v 8.1.

MANUWAL, D. A. ET AL. (Eds) 2001: Biology and conservation of the Common Murre in California, Oregon, Washington, and British Columbia. Volume 1: Natural history and population trends. U.S. Geological Survey, Biological Resources Division, Information and Technology Report, Washington, D.C. 132 pp.

SCHÖNWETTER M. 1960-1992: Handbuch der Oologie, Vol. 1: 464.

# 5. The eggs of the Common Cuckoo

---

*The Common Cuckoo does not build nests, but lays its eggs in nests of songbirds. To be incubated by the host bird, the female cuckoo must lay eggs that match the eggs of the host species. This reproduction strategy is called brood parasitism. Female cuckoos cannot consciously adapt their eggs to those of the host bird. They always lay their eggs in the nests of the species which raised them. As there are different species of host birds, there are also cuckoos specialized in different host birds. They are all members of the same species, but laying different types of eggs.*

**Taxonomy**
There are 136 cuckoo species, divided into 28 genera. The Common Cuckoo belongs to the family of the *Cuculidae* and to the genus *Cuculus* which includes 10 species. The Common Cuckoo (*Cuculus canorus*) is the only of the 136 species found in Central Europe.

**The eggs of the Common Cuckoo**
As has been said, female cuckoos are specialized in a certain species of host birds. Therefore, different cuckoos lay eggs of different colors and patterns. But each individual female cuckoo can only lay eggs in one coloration and pattern, and this throughout her life. If, for instance, the host bird lays white or blue eggs, the cuckoo eggs are also white or blue and match the eggs of the host bird almost perfectly. If the cuckoo has to mimic spotted eggs, the result is sometimes perfect and sometimes less satisfactory (see figure 14 and 15). The specialization in certain species of host birds has an effect on both the appearance and the size of the egg. As a result, the cuckoo generally lays smaller eggs than other birds of the same adult body mass. Nonetheless, a cuckoo egg is usually bigger than the egg of its host birds. But if a host bird lays very small eggs, such as the Wren, the cuckoo egg is also correspondingly smaller.

*Figure 14: Cuckoo egg (left) together with the egg of his host bird*
*The eggs are shown in original size. Please note that the cuckoo egg is smaller in case of the Great Grey Shrike as host bird.*

An average egg of the Common Cuckoo has the following characteristics:
- Length: 22.3 mm
- Width: 16.5 mm

- Volume: 3.10 ml
- Weight: 3.22 g
- Eggshell weight: 0.23 g
- Eggshell thickness: 0.10 mm

But an egg of the Common Cuckoo laid in a Wren's nest, measures 21.1 × 15.8 mm and is, in relation to the weight of the average egg, almost 14% smaller.

## Types of the Common Cuckoo

Genes regulating egg coloration and size are located on a female-specific chromosome. Therefore, the male cuckoo is not host-specific. The female cuckoos can be divided in different types, which can be assigned to certain groups of host birds. But all female cuckoos look the same and belong to the same species. In table 12, some types of the female Common Cuckoo are listed which are specialized either in a certain group or in a certain genus of songbirds.

*Table 12: Types of Common Cuckoos specialized in particular groups of host birds*

| Cuckoo types specialized in | Examples of host birds |
| --- | --- |
| certain songbirds laying blue eggs | Redstart |
| | Dunnock |
| | Whinchat |
| certain songbirds laying white eggs | Black Redstart |
| | Wren |
| songbirds of the genus pipits | Meadow Pipit |
| | Tree Pipit |
| warblers of the genus *Sylvia* | Garden Warbler |
| | Eurasian Blackcap |
| | Common Whitethroat |
| warblers of the genus *Acrocephalus* | Reed Warbler |
| | Sedge Warbler |
| | Marsh Warbler |
| shrikes of the genus *Lanius* | Red-backed Shrike |
| | Great Gray Shrike |

**The host birds of the Common Cuckoo**
More than 100 host species have been recorded. The most common are
- in northern Europe: Meadow Pipit, Dunnock, Eur- Reed Warbler,
- in central Europe: Garden Warbler, Meadow Pipit, Pied Wagtail, European Robin,
- in Finland: Brambling, Redstart.

It is difficult to make a final list of all host birds of the Common Cuckoo. It is assumed that a list of common host birds includes about 50 to 60 names. Probably the most prominent host bird is the Reed Warbler.

*Table 13: Some of the most important host birds of the Common Cuckoo*

| Scientific name | |
| --- | --- |
| *Acrocephalus arundinaceus* | Great Reed Warbler |
| *Acrocephalus schoenobaenus* | Sedge Warbler |
| *Acrocephalus palustris* | Marsh Warbler |
| *Acrocephalus scirpaceus* | Reed Warbler |
| *Anthus pratensis* | Meadow Pipit |
| *Anthus trivialis* | Tree Pipit |
| *Erithacus rubecula* | European Robin |
| *Fringilla montifringilla* | Brambling |
| *Lanius collurio* | Red-backed Shrike |
| *Lanius excubitor* | Great Grey Shrike |
| *Motacilla alba* | Pied Wagtail |
| *Motacilla flava* | Yellow Wagtail |
| *Muscicapa striata* | Spotted Flycatcher |
| *Phoenicurus ochruros* | Black Redstart |
| *Phoenicurus phoenicurus* | Redstart |
| *Phylloscopus sibilatrix* | Wood Warbler |
| *Prunella modularis* | Dunnock |
| *Prunella phoenicurus* | Redstart |
| *Saxicola rubetra* | Whinchat |
| *Sylvia atricapilla* | Eurasian Blackcap |
| *Sylvia borin* | Garden Warbler |
| *Sylvia communis* | Common Whitethroat |
| *Troglodytes troglodytes* | Wren |
| *Turdus merula* | Blackbird |

*Figure 15: Host bird clutches with one egg of the Common Cuckoo*
*Examples of how the cuckoo egg differently matches the host eggs:*
*Top left: Great Reed Warbler*
*Top right: Dunnock*
*Bottom left: Red-backed Shrike*
*Bottom right: Sedge Warbler*

# 6. The penguin eggs

---

*TV programs and feature films have largely contributed to the penguins' popularity. But neither in these media nor in the many richly illustrated penguin books the penguin eggs are described in detail. Penguin eggs are also rare pieces in egg collections.*

**Taxonomy**

The penguin family (Spheniscidae) consists of 18 species and 10 subspecies in six genera *(IOC World Bird List v. 7.3 2017)*. Table 14 shows the 18 species of the *Spheniscidae* family:

*Table 14: Names of the 18 penguin species*

| Common name | Scientific name |
| --- | --- |
| King Penguin | *Aptenodytes patagonicus* |
| Emperor Penguin | *Aptenodytes forsteri* |
| Gentoo Penguin | *Pygoscelis papua* |
| Adélie Penguin | *Pygoscelis adeliae* |
| Chinstrap Penguin | *Pygoscelis antarcticus* |
| Royal Penguin | *Eudyptes schlegeli* |
| Macaroni Penguin | *Eudyptes chrysolophus* |
| Northern Rockhopper Penguin | *Eudyptes moseleyi* |
| Southern Rockhopper Penguin | *Eudyptes chrysocome* |
| Erect-crested Penguin | *Eudyptes sclateri* |
| Fiordland Penguin | *Eudyptes pachyrhynchus* |
| Snares Penguin | *Eudyptes robustus* |
| Yellow-eyed Penguin | *Megadyptes antipodes* |
| Little Penguin | *Eudyptula minor* |
| African Penguin | *Spheniscus demersus* |
| Magellanic Penguin | *Spheniscus magellanicus* |
| Humboldt Penguin | *Spheniscus humboldti* |
| Galapagos Penguin | *Spheniscus mendiculus* |

## Penguin eggs

Depending on the weight of the bird, the eggs differ in size. While the egg of the smallest penguin (*Eudyptula minor*) is similar to a chicken egg, the egg of the largest penguin (*Aptenodytes forsteri*) is more than eight times heavier (see table 15 and 16).

*Table 15: Egg mass and egg-size diphormism (ratio A-egg/B-egg)*

| | Clutch size | A-egg g | B-egg g | Ratio A-egg/ B-egg |
|---|---|---|---|---|
| Aptenodytes patagonicus | 1 | 334 | - | - |
| Aptenodytes forsteri | 1 | 445 | - | - |
| Pygoscelis papua | 2 | 135 | 136 | 0.99 |
| Pygoscelis adeliae | 2 | 122 | 115 | 1.06 |
| Pygoscelis antarctica | 2 | 110 | 107 | 1.03 |
| Eudyptes pachyrhynchus | 2 | 99 | 115 | 0.86 |
| Eudyptes robustus | 2 | 102 | 134 | 0.76 |
| Eudyptes sclateri | 2 | 84 | 155 | 0.54 |
| Eudyptes chrysocome | 2 | 91 | 115 | 0.79 |
| Eudyptes schlegeli | 2 | 100 | 164 | 0.61 |
| Eudyptes chrysolophus | 2 | 95 | 149 | 0.64 |
| Eudyptes moseleyi | 2 | 78 | 108 | 0.72 |
| Megadyptes antipodes | 2 | 137 | 139 | 0.99 |
| Eudyptula minor | 2 | 55 | 55 | 1.0 |
| Spheniscus demersus | 2 | 104 | 101 | 1.03 |
| Spheniscus humboldti | 2 | 121 | 121 | 1.0 |
| Spheniscus magellanicus | 2 | 109 | 109 | 1.0 |
| Spheniscus mendiculus | 2 | 81 | 83 | 0.98 |

16 of the 18 penguin species lay two eggs per clutch. The two largest species (*Aptenodytes*) have a one-egg clutch. The nine species of the genus *Pygoscelis*, *Spheniscus*, *Megadyptes* and *Eudyptula* have a two-egg clutch with nearly equal-sized eggs. The genus *Eudyptes*, however, exhibits an extreme degree of egg size diphormism, where the first-laid A-egg is 18% to 46% lighter in weight than the second-laid B-egg (see table 15). Such an extreme egg-size diphormism is unique in the avian fauna

and may be interpreted as a transitional stage in the evolution towards a one-egg clutch.

Most penguin species incubate their eggs on hard substrates with little nesting material – circumstances that could easily lead to egg breakage. But studies have shown that penguin eggs rarely break or crack. This is because penguins have thicker eggshells. For example, the thickness of the eggshell of Emperor Penguin (*Aptenodytes forsteri*) is 1.08 mm. This shell is nearly 30% thicker than the average eggshell of a bird with the same egg mass. In figure 16, the shell thickness for 12 penguin species is plotted versus their egg mass (SCHÖNWETTER 1960-1992). In addition, a curve was added showing the average shell thickness as a function of the egg mass for all bird families. The shell values for the penguins are at least 15% higher than the typical values for bird eggs of similar weight.

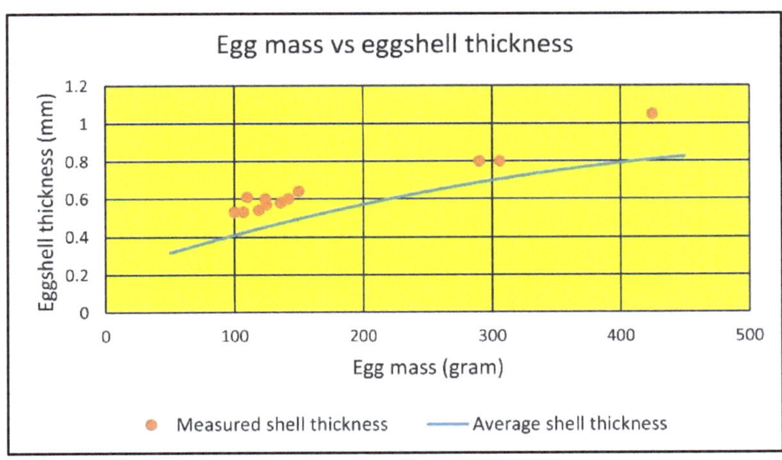


*Figure 16: Eggshell thickness as a function of the egg mass*
*Blue curve: average values for all bird families*
*Orange data points: measured values for penguin eggs (12 species)*

In museum collections, penguin eggs are white or slightly brownish (stained from nesting material). The freshly laid eggs can show different colors, e. g. bluish (*Megadyptes antipodes*). This coloration often disappears a few days after oviposition.

*Table 16: Egg dimensions*
*Where A-eggs and B-eggs are different, the dimension of the larger egg is listed.*

| | Egg length mm | Egg width mm | Ratio L/W* |
|---|---|---|---|
| Aptenodytes patagonicus | 106 | 76 | 1.39 |
| Aptenodytes forsteri | 119 | 82 | 1.45 |
| Pygoscelis papua | 70 | 59 | 1.19 |
| Pygoscelis adeliae | 70 | 56 | 1.25 |
| Pygoscelis antarctica | 68 | 54 | 1.21 |
| Eudyptes pachyrhynchus | 71 | 54 | 1.31 |
| Eudyptes robustus | 74 | 57 | 1.30 |
| Eudyptes sclateri | 80 | 58 | 1.38 |
| Eudyptes chrysocome | 71 | 54 | 1.32 |
| Eudyptes schlegeli | 82 | 60 | 1.37 |
| Eudyptes chrysolophus | 77 | 59 | 1.31 |
| Eudyptes moseleyi | 69 | 53 | 1.30 |
| Megadyptes antipodes | 77 | 57 | 1.35 |
| Eudyptula minor | 56 | 42 | 1.33 |
| Spheniscus demersus | 69 | 52 | 1.33 |
| Spheniscus humboldti | 72 | 55 | 1.31 |
| Spheniscus magellanicus | 70 | 53 | 1.32 |
| Spheniscus mendiculus | 62 | 49 | 1.27 |

** factor k according to SCHÖNWETTER (see text)*

The shape varies among genera and species. The *Pygoscelis* eggs are nearly round, while the *Aptenodytes* eggs are cone-shaped. SCHÖNWETTER (1960-1992) introduced a factor k (defined as the ratio of the long and the wide eggshell axis, see table 16) which describes the degree of roundness. With higher values of k the shape turns from round to elliptic.

Aptenodyptes patagonicus       Aptenodyptes forsteri

*Figure 17: The eggs of the largest penguins:*
*Emperor Penguin (right) and King Penguin*

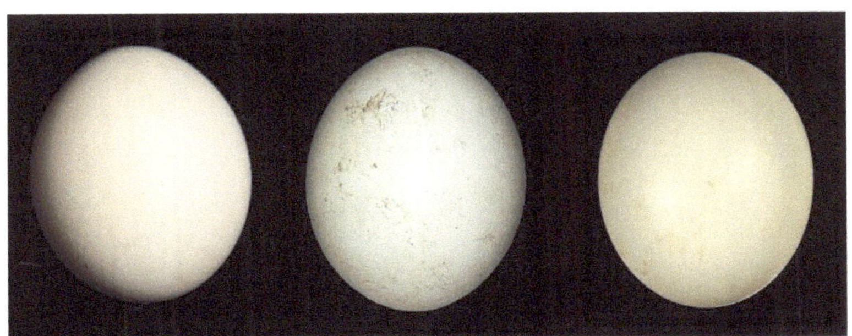

Pygoscelis      Pygoscelis      Pygoscelis
papua        adeliae        antarctica

*Figure 18: The eggs of the genus Pygoscelis from left:*
*Gentoo Penguin*
*Adelie Penguin*
*Chinstrap Penguin*

*Figure 19: The eggs of the genus Eudyptes (crested pen-*
*guins) from top left:*
*Fiordland Penguin*
*Snares Penguin*
*Erect-crested Penguin*
*Southern Rockhopper Penguin*
*Royal Penguin*
*Macaroni Penguin*
*Northern Rockhopper Penguin*

*Figure 20: Eggs of (from top left to bottom right):*
*Yellow-eyed Penguin*
*Little Penguin*
*African Penguin*
*Humboldt Penguin*
*Magellanic Penguin*
*Galapagos Penguin*

*Figure 21: The largest and the smallest penguin egg compared to a chicken egg*


**Reference**
SCHÖNWETTER M. 1960-1992: Handbuch der Oologie. Vol.
1: 47-51

# 7. Kiwi eggs

*The kiwis are known in the avian fauna, because they lay the largest eggs in relation to the adult body mass. (This is not exactly true. See below for details.) In addition, kiwi eggs are hardly available, as only six zoos outside New Zealand keep kiwis which lay eggs. And a kiwi egg may only be exported from New Zealand after approval by the Department of Conservation.*

**Taxonomy**
The Kiwi family (*Apterygidae*) consists of five species and two subspecies in one genus (see table 17).

*Table 17: Apterygidae (IOC World Bird List v 8.1, 2018)*

| Common name | Species | Subspecies |
|---|---|---|
| Southern Brown Kiwi | *Apteryx australis* | |
| Southern Brown Kiwi (South Island) | | *Apteryx australis australis* |
| Southern Brown Kiwi (Stewart Island) | | *Apteryx australis lawryi* |
| North Island Brown Kiwi | *Apteryx mantelli* | |
| Okarito Kiwi | *Apteryx rowi* | |
| Little Spotted Kiwi | *Apteryx owenii* | |
| Great Spotted Kiwi | *Apteryx haastii* | |

**Kiwi eggs**
The weight of kiwi eggs varies between 310 g and 469 g, which is roughly equivalent to the weight of five to eight chicken eggs (see table 18). The following formula can be used with sufficient accuracy to calculate the weight $W$ (g) from the length $L$ and the width $B$ (cm):
$W = 0.56 \times L \times B^2$

A noteworthy characteristic of kiwi eggs is their size in relation to the body weight of the female hen. Very small birds, e.g. some species of hummingbirds, lay eggs whose size amounts up to 15% of the bird weight. For some species of seabirds and shorebirds (e.g. *Oceanites oceanicus*), their eggs weighing 10 grams can even amount up to 30% of the female body weight. However, as the size of the bird increases, this ratio decreases and amounts only 1.6% for the largest extant bird species, the Common Ostrich. In case of the Little Spotted Kiwi, the egg size in relation to the bird's body mass is insofar exceptional, as the egg weight exceeds 300 gram and makes up 23% of the female body weight. In single cases, this value can even amount to 27%.

For the four larger kiwi species this ratio is less extreme, but still 13 to 17% (see table 18) which is far more than what is typical for birds of the same body mass. As a comparison: The body mass of a domestic chicken hen is about the same as for the Southern Brown Kiwi. But its egg (weighing 60 grams) is less than one seventh of the egg of a Southern Brown Kiwi weighing 446 grams.

*Figure 22: Kiwi with egg compared to a domestic chicken with egg*

*Table 18: Characteristics of kiwi eggs compared to an average chicken egg*

| Species | Egg dimension L x B mm | Volume V (ml) | Egg mass W (g) | Female body mass B (kg) | Ratio % Egg mass/ body mass | Egg-shell thickness d (mm) |
|---|---|---|---|---|---|---|
| Apteryx mantelli | 127 × 79 (N= 66) | 414 | 438 | 2.51 (N=31) | 17.5% | 0.50 |
| Apteryx rowi | 126 × 79 | 411 | 440 | 2.65 (N=51) | 16.6% | |
| Apteryx owenii | 109 × 71 (N=9) | 287 | 310 | 1.35 (N=41) | 23.0% | |
| Apteryx haastii | 123 × 78 (N=3) | 419 | 428 | 3.19 (N=29) | 13.4% | 0.52 |
| Apteryx australis | 130 × 81 (N=14) | 446 | 469 | 3.115 (N=10) | 15.1% | 0.5 |
| Gallus gallus domesticus | 57 × 43 | 55.2 | 60 | 3.0* | 2.0% | |

*N = number of measured birds or eggs*
** A domestic chicken laying a 60 gram egg can have a body mass between 1.5 kg and 4.0 kg. For this comparison, a value of 3.0 kg is chosen.*

Kiwi eggs have an almost elliptical shape with an axial ratio (length divided by width) of about 1.6. Therefore, the egg volume $V$ (ml) can be calculated very precisely from the length $L$ (cm) and the width $B$ (cm) using the following formula:

$$V = 0.5236 \times L \times B^2$$

The egg color is pale green for the kiwi species *A. mantelli* and *A. owenii* and white for the species *A. rowi* and *A. haastii*. The species *A. australis* has also white eggs, but for the population living on Stewart Island the eggshell color is pale green. Most kiwi eggs in museum collections look yellowish to brownish.

*Figure 23: Kiwi eggs*
*Top left: Okarito Kiwi*
*Top right: Little Spotted Kiwi*
*Bottom left: Southern Brown Kiwi*
*Bottom right: North Island Brown Kiwi*

*Figure 24: Egg of the Great Spotted Kiwi compared to an egg of a domestic chicken*

**References**

JOLLY J.N., CH. H. DAUGHERTY 2002: Comparison of Little Spotted Kiwi (*Apteryx owenii*) from Kapiti and D'Urville Islands. In Science and research internal report, pp. 57-64, Wellington, New Zealand: Department of Conservation.

JOLLY J.N. 1989: A field study of the breeding biology of the Little Spotted Kiwi (*Apteryx owenii*) with emphasis on the causes of nest failures. Journal of the Royal Society of New Zealand, 19(4): 433-448.

MCLENNAN J.A.,A. J. MCCANN 1991: Ecology of Great Spotted Kiwi, *Apteryx haastii*. DSIR Land Resources Contract Report No. 91/48 (unpublished). DSIR, Lower Hutt. 36 p.

MCLENNAN J. A.,A. J. MCCANN 2002: Genetic Variability, Distribution and Abundance of Great Spotted Kiwi (*Apteryx haastii*). Wellington, New Zealand: Department of Conservation.

REID B. 1971: The Weight of the Kiwi and its Egg. Notornis 18(4): 245-49.

REID B. 1971: Composition of a Kiwi Egg. Notornis 18(4): 250-52.

REID B. 1981: Size Discrepancy between Eggs of Wild and Captive Brown Kiwi (*Apteryx Australis Mantelli*). Notornis 28(4): 281-287.

REID B. 1981: Estimating the Fresh Weight of the Eggs of Brown Kiwi (*Apteryx Australis Mantelli*). Notornis 28(4): 288-91.

REID B. 1972: Kiwi eggs laid at Wellington Zoo. Notornis, 19(3): 276-277.

SALES J. 2005: The endangered kiwi: a review. Folia Zool. 54(1–2): 1-20.

SCHÖNWETTER M. 1960-1992: Handbuch der Oologie, Vol. 1: 35-37.

# About the author

---

**Kurt Schläpfer**, now retired, was scientist in an institute for materials testing and research. In this capacity, he has written a textbook on color theory and color measurement. The egg collection of his wife Béatrice inspired him to study the colors of avian eggs. After a scientific publication on this topic, he and his wife wrote various brochures on bird eggs (see www.natureier.ch).

*The author, Kurt Schläpfer, measuring the color of a casso-wary egg*

www.ingramcontent.com/pod-product-compliance
Lightning Source LLC
Chambersburg PA
CBHW040301240726
48664CB00006B/1330